An
Approximately True
Analysis
of
FAKE NEWS

The Book of Lying and Propaganda

First published in the UK 2018
An Approximately True Analysis of Fake News
ISBN   9781854570963
Published by: Clinical Press Ltd., Redland Green Farm, Redland, Bristol, BS6 7HF, UK. www.clinicalpress.co.uk

Other Books by Paul R Goddard published by Clinical Press Ltd.

Documentary/Non-Fiction authored/edited by Paul R Goddard

- *The History of Medicine, Money and Politics: Riding the Rollercoaster of State Medicine*
- *The National Elf Service: Not the NHS*
- *Bristol Medico-Historical Proceedings Volumes 6 and 7*

Fiction (Paperback and/or ebook form) **Thrillers:**
The Sacrifice Game: El Juego del Sacrificio

- *The Confessions of Saul* • *The Writing on the Wall* • *Reincarnation*

In production

- *The Fellowship of the Egg,* • *Caliphate* • *Echoes of Retribution*
- *The Order of the Salmon*

Fantasy:
The fantasy books all inter-relate but are separate complete stories

The Witch, the Dragon and the Angel Trilogy

- *Witch Way Home?,* • *Witch Armageddon? and* • *Witch Schism and Chaos?* plus two more (it's a magical trilogy!)
- *Tsunami* • *Change* and a prequel • *Parsifal's Pact*

The Witches' Brew Trilogy:

- *Hubble Bubble* • *Toil* • *Trouble*

On a similar theme

- *Oberon's Bane*
- *Parables from Parallel Places: An Anthology of Poetry*
- *Ghost Train: An Anthology of Short Stories*

Fantasy Thrillers in production

- *This Skin And The Next* and • *No Blood From a Stone*

An
Approximately True
Analysis
of
FAKE NEWS

The Book of Lying and Propaganda

Paul R Goddard

Foreword by Chris Beetles

Contents

Foreword

Paul Goddard is nothing if not witty and somehow he manages to be both. So please take my advice; by all means read this comic book Fake News, give in to the laughter which comes unbidden and irresistible like an ageing fart, and then just throw it away. Do not slip case it and lodge it between the sets of Dickens and Austen in their quarter bound morocco leather. This book is worthless and subversive and deserves to be shredded. Resist temptation to give it as a jolly present to your friends on the thin assumption that a chortling belly laugh will make them feel better.

We live in an age of great seriousness when we should support and revere our great leaders and not lampoon and satirise. Stop mocking the great even if they are corrupt and divisive. Please tell me what good does laughter ever achieve?

Really?!

Well I disagree.

Paul is a very funny and energetic clown, but honestly he is a retired doctor for God's sake, and should give up his role as the court jester of Somerset and Avon and get back to handing out prescriptions for Amoxicillin.

All right, all right, have it your way .. enjoy this very funny book if you must, read it three times a day after meals, but don't say I didn't warn you when you feel a whole lot better.

Chris Beetles

Chris Beetles Gallery
8-10 Ryder St, St. James's, London SW1Y 6QB, UK

5

Acknowledgements

Even a book as short as this one requires more than just an author and I would like to acknowledge the help I have received from so many people.

First and foremost I would like to thank my wife, Lois, for her encouragement and unfailing support. In addition many thanks to both my sons and to my friends Donald Bradford, Jeremy Mann and Evelyn Smith for proofreading the manuscript and advice regarding the cover.

Peter Dougill very kindly gave me tips on drawing the cartoons and I am grateful to Chris Beetles for writing the foreword.

Thank you to Clinical Press for publishing my work, to Book Printing UK for their excellent printing and Gazelle Book Services for distributing the books.

Finally I am delighted that you, the reader, have given up your time to look at my humble offering *(creep, creep. Ed.)*. Many thanks!

Paul Goddard

Introduction

When my son was three years old he was playing with a toy car on the dining room floor at his grandmother's house. A stream of expletives, presumably learnt from us, was emanating from his mouth.

'What did you say?' his grandmother cried, shocked to hear such words from a small child.

'It's not me, Granny,' he replied. 'It's the jeep driver!'

The cartoon above illustrates the story. Now in our family any time anyone makes a feeble excuse, something that no-one could possibly believe, we invoke the ghost of the jeep driver. So that is what this book is about: role playing, posturing, propaganda and, yes, lying. In two words; fake news.

The cartoon does not look like my son. Yeah, I faked it so that it was funnier.

Donald Trump reminds me of that three year old child. His lies are clearly unbelievable but he does not seem to notice that very few people believe him or why his fake news is clearly only acceptable to his credulous followers.

Trump did not invent the word fake but he claimed that he did. According to the Pages dictionary its origin was late 18th century, perhaps related to the German fegen meaning to sweep or thrash.

Of course Trump does not have to believe that. All he feels he has to do to discredit something is to declare that it is fake news and the game is over.

Perhaps when he declared that he had invented "fake" he "misspoke" and really meant that he invented the term fake news.

He certainly did not even do that. The word "news" developed from French or Latin and is late Middle English so

"Fake News" as a term to describe propaganda may have been around since the 18th century.

According to Mike Wendling of BBC Trending the modern usage of the term Fake News was developed by Craig Silverman of Buzzfeed who, in mid 2016, noticed a stream of fake stories emanating from a town in Eastern Europe. *"We ended up finding a small cluster of news websites all registered in the same town in Macedonia called Veles,"* Silverman recalls. [1]

Certainly the use of the word fake to denounce false videos (i.e. fake news) was widespread before that. In the comments section on Youtube people took great pleasure in pointing out the way in which the videos had been faked.

In this book we shall examine what fake news is. We shall

look at the development of lying and introduce methods to detect lies. Then the book will give a few examples of fake news from history and others from recent newspapers and other media. Some of the more dangerous examples of fake news will be examined in some detail liberally interspersed with my rather puerile attempts at cartoons.

The President will no doubt help us to do that by popping up whenever I want him to and declaring Fake News!

He looks pleased with that idea!

REFERENCE

1.   *The (almost) complete history of 'fake news' by Mike Wendling BBC Trending https://www.bbc.co.uk/news/blogs-trending-42724320*

Section 1: Propaganda

"Propaganda" was a committee of cardinals of the Roman Catholic Church set up in 1622 by Pope Gregory XV. Their purpose was to be responsible for foreign missions *(Pages Dictionary)* and presumably to combat the Reformation.

In recent years people have focussed on the supposedly recent advent of fake news. This fakery has been propagated through social media and allegedly implicated in the Brexit vote in the United Kingdom and the election of President Trump in the United States of America.

There is, however, nothing really new about fake news except the name and the way in which it is spread. Half a century ago we might simply have called fake news lies or propaganda and in the late 1990s it was termed "spin." Now fake news is also spread by social media and can be started by anyone who wishes to do so. You can start a written blog on your own website or use social media such as Facebook, Twitter, Instagram or Youtube. Or all of them if you wish!

Facebook war room at heart of the fight to halt fake news

Daily Telegraph 19.10.18

The spread of your own propaganda or fake news is facilitated by the little understood algorithms of the social media sites and sometimes *(frequently?)* the fake news is spread for financial gain *(Gosh, is that true? Ed.)*

This book looks at fake news throughout history, how it was propagated and how it can be spotted. We shall examine examples of fake news in a variety of areas of human endeavour including Medicine, Science, Religion, Politics and War, but not necessarily in that order.

Naturally a book like this is bound to annoy people who want to believe the fake news but then again most of the book could be fiction anyway so why get so upset? It is, after all, my little book of lies and propaganda!

Read what I write but believe what you like!

Lying is easy
Lying is fun
But lying's a sin
And should never be done!

Why do people lie? How can we spot the lies?

I made up the rhyme on the opposite page. Did you find yourself nodding in agreement? In fact there is very little truth in it so why did I make it up?

Lying is harder work than telling the truth so why do people do it? Why fake it when it is easier to tell the truth? What is the benefit of lying if it takes more effort?

Convincing lies involve a higher mental function than telling the truth. It is obviously far harder to make something up and remember the fiction than just replaying verbally that which has happened.

Newspapers such as the Daily Sport are full of amusing stories that were made up by the staff and I have it on good authority that they employ some very clever people to make up their fake news ....some say cleverer than the staff at serious papers such as the Times, Daily Telegraph or Grauniad *(surely not! Ed.)*

According to Psychology Today[1] experiments show lying behaviour in children as young as forty-two months *(see the Jeep Driver cartoon on page 7)* but anecdotally it can be observed even earlier.

Talwar and Lee's developmental model of lying [2] suggests that primary lying starts around the age of two to three and is used to hide transgressions. It fails to take into account the mental state of the listener. By the age of four the children tell secondary lies, which are more plausible but still do not cover all available facts and follow up. By seven or eight children learn to tell tertiary lies which are closely consistent with known facts and follow-up statements.

Psychology Today also reminds us that lying is not always negative. Without the ability to fabricate information there

would be no fiction, thus no novels, no Chaucer, Dickens, Brontë, Dumas..... perhaps also no imaginary paintings or sculpture, and very few songs.

How many of the paintings of royalty make the subjects look worse than they did in reality? Precious few is the answer to that question. King Rupert IV, our imaginary king, was painted in an imaginary world where artists do not put out fake news as propaganda for the rulers. Artists purposely flatter their subjects particularly if they are rich, famous or likely to chop off their heads.

Oliver Cromwell (1599–1658), English general and statesman, Lord Protector of the Commonwealth 1653–8, is the exception to that rule, famously insisting that the painting of himself should be truthful.

"Mr Lilly," Cromwell is reputed to have demanded. *"I desire you would use all your skill to paint my picture truly like me, and not flatter me at all but remark all the roughness, pimples, warts and everything as you see me. Otherwise, I will not pay a farthing for it."*

15

It is from his quote that the phrase "warts and all" has developed to mean "including all blemishes." There are, however, many occasions on which it would be inadvisable to tell the ungarnished truth.

Lying is used to gain advantage over other human beings, to ease potentially difficult social situations and to make other people happy. In the cartoon above a famous question is posed and the person answering may be well advised to avoid the truth. It is entirely possible that the ability to lie is necessary if we are to live amicably in close quarters. It becomes a problem when the lying continues in situations that demand the truth, such as the court of law or from people in a position of power, such as politicians or managers.

So lying is fundamental to what makes us human. All that has changed is the ease with which people lie and produce fake news and the way in which the lies are spread

How To Spot Lies (including Fake News)

The development of lying in children does help point out the ways to spot untruths. Spotting a lie requires somewhat differing techniques when a person is perhaps face-to-face with you, on the phone, sending an email or text or the information has been obtained from other social or news media.

Direct Interaction:
- *The Tell*

Poker players will talk about the characteristic which acts as a giveaway when the person they are playing against is faking with regards to their hand. This is known as the "tell".

This in any one individual may be a tic, a tendency to become more animated or more garrulous or some other tell-tale feature such as blushing.

When I was a medical student I heard a story about a patient who had an artificial heart valve implanted but complained afterwards that it had ruined his game of poker. When the room was very quiet the ticking of his heart valve was just audible and if he had a good hand despite keeping a very straight face his increased heart rate served as a giveaway. I told this story to a famous cardiologist when on a ward round with him. The cardiologist, in his superior manner, was not amused and told me that the ticking of the prosthetic valve which I had noted was not the whole story. I was apparently missing some obscure heart murmur which was present as well. Some years later it was I who was entertained when I was told that the cardiologist was most offended by the results of modern imaging techniques which showed that the heart murmurs he espoused to hear

were either imaginary or of little significance and that many of his diagnoses were wrong. The cartoon above was based on the story of the card player with a ticking valve. (Stonewall Jackson was the name of a famous Amercian general, not the actual name of the patient.)

No one can lie, no one can hide anything, when he looks directly into someone's eyes Paulo Coelho (Brazilian Novelist)

This is often believed but unfortunately Coelho is wrong. It is a surprising fact that a good lier will tend to look you in the eyes more frequently when lying than when telling the truth and that people can more easily tell that a person is lying when listening to them on the telephone rather than speaking face-to-face.

18

Analysing Written Information

Look for:

- *Inconsistency*

One of the main difficulties when lying is remaining consistent. That is the reason that the police will continue to question a suspect for long periods of time and a barrister in court will constantly ask the same question but in a different way. It is not that they did not understand or even record the first answer. They wish to see if the witness remains constant in their answers and whether they are able to add extra detail. Sometimes extra detail is added but the embellishment flies in the face of known facts. The suspect has overplayed their hand. When analysing written information it will sometimes be obvious that extra information within the story is not consistent with the original statement.

Half a truth is often a great lie. Benjamin Franklin

Benjamin Franklin was right. A half-truth is more difficult to detect than a downright lie and a good lier will know this. We must remember that just because many of the facts in a statement are true it does not mean that the the crux of the matter is also true.

- *Excessive consistency but no added facts*

One method, if you are lying, is to keep precisely to the original story without altering a word that is said. If the story is repeated parrot fashion it is indicative that the answer has been learnt, as if from a script. In that situation the suspect will add no further corroborating facts. A very bald statement with no corroborating facts should be suspected as being fake.

In scientific and medical circles published papers usually go through a peer review process. This in itself is not a perfect method of establishing whether or not a piece of research is accurate but it is better than no method at all. So medics and scientists tend to believe the articles they read in established journals and disbelieve those in fringe publications. Since new ideas may not make it into the most frequently cited journals it is true to say that progress can be stymied by this process. It is important to keep an open mind and read around the subject but overall peer review and a credible source does help to keep science on an even keel.

But what would I consider to be a source that lacks credibility? Perhaps the best example would be an organisation that already disbelieves an established fact and then provides another message supporting their discredited view. Thus Flat Earth Society information is clearly suspect! Or messages emanating from an organisation that bases all its "facts" on divine revelation.

These days it is fairly simple to check the facts via a plethora of websites. I have frequently found that when I google an unlikely statement there are many websites already pointing out that the supposed fact is fake or a scam and explaining why it is the case.

One should be particularly careful when receiving  information from social media such as Twitter, Facebook etcetera. In particular it is dangerous to pass on information that you cannot personally check. Malcicious posting is sometimes referred to as Trolling, the person who posted the comment being called a Troll. Spam is an unsolicited, undesired, or illegal electronic message.

A Rock Troll with Fake Meat?

A recent headline stated that YouGov had purposely influenced a vote in Iraq. Their employees had allegedly done this by posting fake news on social media. This type of activity is known as *"Astroturfing"*: the laying down of fake grass for commercial purposes.

- *Lack of references and/or quotes*

References and quotes can be checked and can help to substantiate a statement. The converse, a lack of references or quotes, renders the statement less plausible.

Surprisingly there are instances when quotes and references make a statement less plausible. Appealing to the work of Einstein without specific reference or quoting a religious book such as the Koran or the Bible to help substantiate a statement may actually make it less likely to be factual. It is important to check the reference source.

Bad spelling and poor punctuation are indicative of poor proof reading and indicate that there has been little editorial control and oversight of the writing. Poor proofreading can destroy confidence even in information that is accurate.

Questions to ask yourself

- *Is the reverse true?*

It is usually very difficult to prove that something is false. In fact much of the philosophy of science is based on creating a theory and then trying to prove it to be wrong. When answering multiple choice questions (MCQs) in exams I used to ask myself if the reverse was true. For example:

True or False: Acromegaly is usually associated with a small pituitary fossa.

Certainly acromegaly is associated with a pituitary abnormality but in what way?

Acromegaly and gigantism are due to a pituitary tumour producing growth hormone. Such tumours cause enlargement of the pituitary fossa so it is reasonable to conclude that acromegaly is usually associated with an enlarged fossa not a small one.

The same reasoning can often be used when examining facts out there on the media. It is not a complete test of the validity as two opposing facts can both be true..... perhaps acromegaly is occasionally found in patients with a small fossa but it is likely to be a rare finding. Nevertheless it is a useful guide. If the opposite to statement A is true it does diminish the likelihood that statement A is also true.

- *Is this wish fulfillment?*

Hope springs eternal in the human breast: Alexander Pope

Is the supposed fact something that you want to be the case? If it is, be doubly cautious about its validity. We are usually less critical about statements we want to be true than we are about statements that annoy us. We might, for example, be more prepared to accept a statement that some technique or patent medicine can cure us of cancer than a bald statement to the opposite. This is wish fulfillment.

Sex with an ex might help to get over split, say researchers

By Daily Telegraph Reporter

The more optimistic we are feeling the more likely we are to accept statements that provide wish fulfillment. If we are depressed and pessimistic we are less likely to believe statements that provide us with hope even if they are true. In such situations it is important to understand our own emotions when judging the validity of a statement.

- *Does the supposed information contradict normal science or commonsense?*

There are some scientific theories that are so well proven that they are accepted as fact by most scientists. Reworking of the laws of thermodynamics state that you cannot get more energy out of a system than you put in (by way of fuel, potential energy etc.). Hence perpetual motion machines are ruled out, at

This remarkable machine runs on water and air. It never needs refuelling.

least at the macroscopic level at which we live. Quantum mechanics and cosmology are a different matter and need not concern us right here though I shall return to them in a later book.

Do we normally see supernatural creatures manifesting in our daily life and if we did would they be contradicting the laws of science? Does magic work in Basingstoke or Swindon? If you think that it might, would it contradict the laws of science or simple commonsense?

If a statement does contradict normal science or commonsense you should be very wary of it.

One amusing story that has been going the rounds is that the world leaders are shape-changing lizards. This was started by David Icke. I've added one of my drawings here as proof that he is right!

THE TRANSFORMATION OF
PRESIDENT TRUMP

For those who wish to know why the picture was put in here: making the drawing was fun and I bet you looked at it and thought, *"Yes, he does look a lot like a lizard"*. There are, however, no such things as shape-changing lizards masquerading as human beings and in particular I do not believe that Trump turns into an Australian bearded dragon! The whole idea contradicts science and commonsense.

I have also written two sci-fi novels* about shape changing lizards so this represents a plug for the books: it is an advertisement! Two good reasons for not believing the picture.

* *This Skin And The Next* and *No Blood From a Stone*

- *Is the supposed fact logical?*

There are many forms of logic but perhaps the simplest to understand and often the most misused is syllogistic logic following the lines of major premise, minor premise, conclusion. A famous example (*Socrates?ed.*) is:

"All men are mortal

I am a man

Therefore I am mortal"

If the major premise is true and the minor premise is correctly stated the conclusion is certain.

Frequently the major premise is wrong or the minor premise is inverted. In the example above the second line might be changed to read: "I am mortal" leading to the incorrect conclusion "Therefore I am a man". You might be a woman!

Inverted syllogism is frequently resorted to by politicians and religious leaders. Look out for it.

In the example above even the original major premise is suspect. How do we know that all men are mortal? Mortality can only be proven by death and it is certainly not true that we are all dead, otherwise you could not read this sentence.

This does lead onto the logic of statistics. It can be stated that all men, before those presently alive, have eventually died. Thus statistically the likelihood that all men are mortal is very high but not proven. Perhaps advanced medicine will make some immortal!

I shall discuss statistics later in the book.

- *Have you heard exactly the same improbable story with different protagonists?*

If the details in two supposedly unrelated stories are really very similar it would seem probable that one story is borrowing from the other. Many myths are common between different religions and appear to have been borrowed or adapted from one another. Many gods, for example, are reputed to have been born from virgin birth.

- *Does the "fact" rhyme?*

For some psychological reason people are more likely to believe something if it rhymes. Old adages are very frequently in verse form, for example:

Early to bed and early to rise

Makes a man healthy, wealthy and wise.

This is more easily remembered than *"Go to bed early and get up early and you'll be rich, fit and sagacious."* Neither is particularly true but the rhyming one is more likely to be believed. So we should be very wary of "facts" that rhyme. Alliteration, as in *"wealthy and wise"*, is also dangerous and much beloved of demagogues and preachers

Now is the time

To beware of a rhyme!

- *Is This "News" Just a Form of Advertising?*

Obviously this is not the original advertisement because it is protected by copyright but it is a fair approximation.

Doctors never preferred a Camel: that was all fake news and it continued well into the 1950s when smoking as the major cause of lung cancer was well established.

Advertising is a good example of a situation where somebody has financial incentives to provide fake news. Sometimes the advertising is dressed up as "advertorial". The advert looks exactly like the rest of the text in the magazine or newspaper and careful reading is required to realise that what you are perusing is an advert and therefore fake news must be suspected.

From the sale of indulgences to the present day television evangelists there have been people making financial gain out of religious propaganda.

The Pages dictionary states that indulgences were grants from the Pope for remission of purgatory for sins and that their widespread sale by pardoners was a considerable abuse in the Middle Ages. The suggestion that such an indulgence was needed was another example of historical fake news.

A recent pope decreed that purgatory does not exist. More fake news about a non-existent place or condition.

Carol Brooks states [3]

"The church began as a movement in Jerusalem. It became a philosophy in Greece, an institution in Rome, a culture in Europe and, when it came to America, it became a business... a highly profitable business.....

L. Ron Hubbard (Founder of Scientology) once said "Writing for a penny a word is ridiculous. If a man really wanted to make a million dollars, the best way would be to start his own religion." While our modern day evangelists

have not started their own religion, they have unquestionably improved on Hubbard's idea. Capitalizing on Christianity has proved to be far more lucrative than starting a new religion. But as the Bible tells us.. 'evil men and impostors shall wax worse and worse, deceiving and being deceived. [2 Timothy 3:13]'"

- *Is the News Only a Prediction?*

Predictions are often dressed up as the truth. The weather forecasters appear to have learnt their lesson following Michael Fish's embarrassing putdown in 1987 when he stated that there was no hurricane on the way. Nowadays they give a percentage likelihood of rain or just state that it is likely, or just a possibility.

Other punters are not so careful. In the financial pages look for the statement that investments can go down as well as up: that means that the article is an advertorial.

Copper trade to surge as China's global lending fuels demand

The above headline was in the Daily Telegraph. But is it true? A subtitle noted that the information was from miner* BHP Billiton....and they, of course, have a reason to push the idea that copper trade will surge. Other sources on the internet on the same date tell me that copper is in a bear market so this was a typical example of fake news!

   * they meant mining company, not miners.

In the financial sections and the sports pages predictions are rife and often dressed up as news.

Don't forget this: predictions are all fake news unless or until they are proved right. Consider who might benefit from the prediction coming true.

An Intelligence Officer's Telltale Signs

The preceding points were my own observations but from News.com.au[(4)], reporting on an article in the Wall Street Journal, intelligence officer Tyler Cohen Wood came up with seven telltale signs that someone is lying. They do overlap with my own pointers but I think they are so good that I have directly quoted them below:

1. Emphatic Language

It doesn't necessarily mean he or she is lying, but rather that he or she really wants you to believe what is being said. This is also the case when a person keeps saying the same thing over and over in slightly different ways.

2. Distant Language

In person, someone may unconsciously distance himself by crossing his arms in front of him. In writing, he can achieve this same effect by omitting personal pronouns and references to himself.

3. Unanswered questions

You ask, and the other person hedges or changes the subject. Most likely, the person doesn't like saying no, or doesn't want to hurt your feelings. But he or she may also be keeping something from you.

4. Non-committal statements

Noncommittal statements are red flags — 'pretty sure', 'probably', 'must have' and, my least favourite, 'maybe'.

5. Qualifying statements

Cohen Wood says these expressions — 'to be honest', 'there is nothing to worry about', 'I hate to tell you this' — are often signals that the person is uncomfortable with his or her next statement.

6. Tense hopping

Someone describing an event that happened in the past usually uses the past tense. But if midway through the story the person starts fabricating, that material plays out in his or her head and leads to a switch to the present tense.

7. Uncharacteristic Language

It helps to know a person's baseline behaviour — certain words, phrases and punctuation he or she uses often, and the amount of time he or she tends to take when replying. Pay attention when any of this deviates from the norm. Did someone who is usually chatty and full of details suddenly become curt or vague? Did a quiet person turn into a chatter box?

Fakery in Photography

The camera never lies,

Seeing is believing

and

It has to be seen to be believed

The three aphorisms above show how much we believe the things we see. It is, however, obvious that since the advent of Photoshop it is easier than ever to create false images. Nowadays most people know that it is very easy to fake images. Despite knowing that fake photographs are common, people are still fooled by even the poorest of fakes. The phrases *"seeing is believing"* and *"It has to be seen to be believed"* are both rhymes so one should be wary of accepting them.

Our eyes are easily deceived would be a more accurate saying.

There have, historically, been some very famous fake pictures and recently some of the most famous hoax

Bidding for hoax photos is away with the fairies

photographs sold at auction for a total of more than £20,000. These were the fake fairies pictured by 16-year old Elsie Wright and her nine-year-old cousin Frances Griffiths. Using coloured paper cut-outs and hat pins they staged scenes near the stream in their garden. Whilst Elsie's father was always convinced they were a hoax their mother did believe in the fairies and took the pictures to the Theosophical Society, fooling such luminaries as Arthur Conan Doyle.

This is a little picture of myself, the author, away with the fairies. This was produced using Photoshop. I drew the fairies for John Harvey's excellent book for children called *The Opposite Stone* and I'm hoping that someone will want to pay £20,000 for this really fake picture of the magical kingdom (or perhaps just buy John's book?).

Other famous photographic hoaxes of the last century include The Loch Ness Monster images and Stalin, who had his henchmen airbrushed out of photographs whenever they fell from favour (and mostly were executed).

Fakery by mistake

Communication between human beings is never perfect and there are many occasions when a message is garbled and becomes fake news.

Famously and possibly apocryphally is the message sent in the First World War from the front: *"Send reinforcements we are going to advance"* which became *"Send three and fourpence we are going to a dance."*

This is the basis of a game known (with considerable political incorrectness) as Chinese Whispers. One person whispers something in someone's ear and they must pass on to the next person that which they think they heard and so on, round the room until it comes back to the first person and the two quite disparate messages are shouted out, to much jollity and laughter. The game does not work at all well with older people (like myself) as we all say, very loudly, things such as *'Speak up, I couldn't hear you,'* and then proceed to immediately shout out the message we have just heard.

13 places in Bristol you didn't know were haunted

Fake by mistake or just good marketing? B24/7 (http://www.bristol247.com)

The headline above amused me. Since, in my opinion, ghosts are highly unlikely to exist the writer of the headline and article is mistaken. It is true that I did not know they were haunted because it is highly improbable that they are! But the places mentioned, such as the Llandoger Trow, SS Great Britain and the Old Vic are well worth visiting and do have gory stories of murder and betrayal.

Can headlines always be believed?

Finally in this section there is Betteridge's law of headlines that states that "Any headline that ends in a question mark can be answered by the word no."[5]

REFERENCES

1. *https://www.psychologytoday.com/us/blog/media-spotlight/201311/when-does-lying-begin)*
2. *Talwar V, Lee K. Development of lying to conceal a transgression: Children's control of expressive behavior during verbal deception. International Journal of Behavioral Development. 2002;26:436–444. doi: 10.1080/01650250143000373*
3. *http://www.inplainsite.org/html/tele-evangelist_lifestyles.html*
4. *https://www.news.com.au/technology/online/how-to-tell-if-someone-is-lying-to-you-online-or-in-a-text/news-story/f76033116da0964f-2565d5a0d0180812*
5. *https://en.wikipedia.org/wiki/Betteridge%27s_law_of_headlines*

The citizens of Jericho refuse to hand over their city to Joshua

Julius Caesar

Julius Caesar in Britain?

Section 2:
Some Famous Historical Lies

History is written by the victors: Winston Churchill

"It ain't what you don't know that gets you into trouble. It's what you know for sure that just ain't so": incorrectly attributed to Mark Twain

On the opposite page are my cartoons of two famous incidents that are purported to be historical. At the top is the story of Joshua and the battle of Jericho. I have drawn the picture from the perspective of the defenders rather than the usual view with the walls tumbling and the celebrating Israelites. Now my grouse about this story is not that the walls magically collapsed, it seems that the walls of Jericho did indeed collapse due to an earthquake: variously viewed as God-given or natural. No, my argument with the story, as usually related, is that the peace-loving citizens of Jericho had locked themselves into the city but Joshua and the hordes killed the lot of them except the family of a harlot who had betrayed the city dwellers. We are supposed to think of Joshua as a great hero?

There can be no more fertile ground for fake news than the world of politicians. Throughout history the view of the winning side in any conflict has been the one that dominates the ongoing story. Politicians, be they noblemen and royalty of the past or the statesmen of the present, will present their own case in the most glowing light whilst denigrating their worthless opponents. When two sides are in conflict the broadcasts or writings of one side are viewed by the other as being unfounded propaganda. This is simply another word for fake news.

"Veni, vidi, vici". This phrase, which translates as *"I came, I saw, I conquered,"* is often attributed incorrectly to Julius

37

Caesar after he landed in Britain. In fact, according to the Greek historian Appian, Caesar used the phrase in a letter to the Roman Senate about a completely different battle against Pharnaces II of Pontus.

The impression given to schoolchildren is that Caesar's expeditions to our island were a great success and that he conquered Britain. Whilst it is true that some of the chieftains of Celtic Britain may have agreed to trade with the Romans it is also a fact that any small battles he did win were as nought compared with the vastly larger mass of people and land that he had absolutely no sway over. Julius Caesar did not conquer Britain but generations of schoolchildren learning history have been convinced that he did.

Caesar appeared in 55BC, left and returned in 54 BC promptly to leave again and the Brits continued to rule themselves until Claudius invaded in 43AD. The opposite was therefore true, Julius Caesar had not really conquered and since the saying rhymes and uses alliteration it is immediately suspect.

If a lie is repeated frequently enough it becomes accepted as truth. This was apparent to Goebbels, Hitler's Minister of Propaganda. He was the man who had control of the press, radio, and all aspects of culture in Germany throughout the 1930s and until 1945.

He was not the first to notice this and people have been exploiting this fact since the beginning of known history and presumably well before. Goebbels was adept at using the new media of radio and film for propaganda purposes. Comparison can be made with some modern politicians who have very quickly adapted to the world of blogging, Twitter and Facebook.

On the opposite page is a picture of Queen Elizabeth I.

She was reputed to be a virgin wedded to her country but some people believe that she gave birth to two or even three children. When I put this to a friend of mine he laughed and asked me how she could possibly have done that without anyone knowing. My reply is that they would have known but they would not have dared mention it. *Sir Francis Bacon* by P M Dunn is good further reading on the subject.

My drawing of Queen Elizabeth looks much like the sort you might get in a children's "colouring in" book. If you are getting bored with the text why not take some felt tip pens and colour in a few pictures?

Equality

One dangerous lie that is constantly repeated is an example of wishful thinking. It was propagated by the founders of the United States of America and repeated in the Gettysburg Address and also by the leaders of the French Revolution. At the time that they presented the lie it must have seemed to be a very revolutionary thought but now it is part of Western liberal thinking . What is the lie? One of the most common versions is written out below:

All men are created equal

In the Gettysburg Address of 1863 Abraham Lincoln stated *"Fourscore and seven years ago our fathers brought forth, on this continent, a new nation, conceived in liberty, and dedicated to the proposition that all men are created equal."*

Note that it is gender biased and does not include women except, possibly, as a subset of men. But even worse than

Which is more true: All men are equal or each person is unique?

the gender omission is the fact that it is completely untrue. Nothing could be further from the truth.

To make it more believable it is often dressed up:

All men are born equal

All are equal in the eyes of God

All are equal in the eyes of the law.

Not one of these aphorisms is a fact. Trying to make it a fact has led to wars and revolution.

People are not born equal. That much is obvious to all doctors and midwives. Some are born into a life of luxury and ease, others to abject poverty. Some are born with perfect health and live long lives. Some are born with congenital diseases and die within hours and others are, unfortunately, stillborn. There is every conceivable variation between these two extremes and none of the babies are equal.

41

Even the act of birth is in no way equal. Some mothers die in labour. Sometimes labour is long, protracted and dangerous and the baby suffers birth trauma. Some babies are born by caesarean section, skillfully conducted and have an almost trauma free entry into this world. Some babies, a decreasing number in the Western world, have a trouble-free normal birth after a short labour.

Then the upbringing starts, creating more inequality. Some have good food, modern healthcare and excellent home-life and education. Others are born in a ghetto, suffer deprivation and no education.

I tried out my scribbled cartoon on my seven-year-old grandson and he instantly replied *'Each person is unique.'*

'Stop,' I hear you cry. *'The saying is metaphysical. It refers to the human soul. Every human soul is equal. That's what it means. It is not a physical thing.'*

The answer is nonsense because we don't even know if souls exist. If, for a moment, we accept the proposition that the soul does exist, who has decided that every human soul is equal? Do we have to invoke a god at this point or some

divine judgement where the soul is weighed against a feather? Is the soul of a monstrous dictator such as Josef Stalin equal to that of a famous artist such as Michelangelo or a writer such as Dickens?

We should ask what form of judgement decides that they are equal?

Is there equality in the Bible?

Some people may resort to a holy book such as the Bible. Leaving to one side, for now, the very real possibility that the holy book may be wrong let us see whether the Bible does say that all men are equal in the eyes of God or, even if it does, if there are verses suggesting exactly the opposite.

Romans 2:11 For God does not show favouritism

This does seem to imply some form of equality but the following verses suggest the opposite:

John 13:16 Very truly I tell you, no servant is greater than his master, nor is a messenger greater than the one who sent him

And

Matthew 22:14 (KJV) For many are called, but few are chosen.

And in the verses above I have not resorted to quoting the Old Testament which has many frightening sections in which people are destroyed, even down to the smiting of first born babies, simply in order to help God's "chosen people". Where is the equality in that?

Is it true politically or by the law?

"..all men are created equal."

The country that produced the Gettysburg Address, which includes such a saying, also kept people in slavery for far longer than Britain, which did not push the revolutionary cant.

Does the law treat people equally? Clearly not. If you are rich you can afford the very best lawyers and perhaps even get away with murder. The names of various famous people might come to mind at this point?

43

If there is nothing to support the statement the conclusion has to be that the original aphorism is wrong. The suggestion that all men are equal is not true and is simply an example of wishful thinking, political imagining and fake news.

Each person is unique. They are not equal and should not be measured in that way.

Does that mean that people should keep to their position in society, follow a course set by a caste or class system? I do not believe that either. Providing fair opportunity which is as equal as possible is to be applauded and believing in the unique nature of each human being will make you value people more rather than believing, incorrectly, that all persons are equal. Fairness rather than equality should be the code. It is not a metaphysical soul-searching creed. It is simply an enaction of the golden rule: *do as you would be done by*. Living by the golden rule does tend to lead to better co-operation and happier lives so why don't we try it more often?

Inalienable Human Rights

Three years go we visited the Museum for Human Rights in Winnipeg, Canada. We walked all round the museum marvelling at the architecture and enjoying the exhibits. Particularly of interest was a travelling exhibition which included an original version of the Magna Carta document and another of the Charter of the Forest. The former gave rights to the Barons and the latter extended rights to the common people, protecting common land and permitting access to the forests by free men. Indeed special courts relating to such rights still exist in the New Forest and the Forest of Dean. One major innovation was the right of a widow to retain her own property and not be forced to marry a relative of the dead husband.

(Note: We met Rupert IV earlier in the book (page 15). In case such a repetition bores you I have coloured him in using felt tips. I've done the same to the telephone box on page 14.)

These documents were the first to give rights to noblemen and to commoners rather than to royalty.

The French and British royalty had already given themselves rights, decreeing that they ruled by divine right, god-given and absolute. I say British rather than just English because the Scottish royalty, the Stuarts, continued to believe this long after the English and when James VI of the Scots became James I of England he brought the tradition back to England, leading eventually to the civil war, the loss of Charles the First's head and, in 1688, the Glorious Revolution and the exile of the Stuarts.

The French continued with the same, amazingly incorrect, belief until finally Louis XVI in 1793 had his head chopped off with the guillotine. They also believed that they could cure people suffering from Tuberculosis in the neck, known as Scrofula. More about that later.

In the twentieth century the rise of workers' rights went unchecked in Britain until the advent of Margaret Thatcher. I've yet to meet anyone who admits to having voted for her despite the fact that she became the longest-serving British Prime Minister of the 20th century, elected each time by landslide victories. Her reforms went too far and workers' rights have been undermined.

Since then rights have (apparently) been extended to all the people in the European Union. This is, on the face of it, a very good thing.

Britain is signed up to the European Convention on Human Rights. Unfortunately the most high-profile human rights cases have been those of preachers of hate demanding that they are not deported back to their country of origin as it might impact on their right to have a family life or that the country in question will not give them their basic human

rights. The missing human rights might, for example, include disability benefits and treatment: disabilities brought on by making and exploding bombs. But what about the rights of the human beings affected by the preaching of the person in question? Do the human rights of one individual trump the rights of myriad others just because they have employed a lawyer? Who pays for that lawyer?

The Animal Liberation Front some years ago in Bristol nearly killed a child by setting off a bomb.

The militant protesters seem to forget that human beings are animals.

The Canadian Museum for Human Rights

So this brings me to the point of this section.

There is no such thing as an inalienable right.

Yes. You read it correctly. It is fake news put out there by politicians and human rights lawyers. The rights have been created by law makers and can only be maintained by someone taking responsibility for their enaction.

So back we go to the Canadian Museum for Human Rights in Winnipeg, mentioned a few pages ago. In the entire museum was there any mention of human responsibilities?

Human rights, yes. Human responsibilities, no.

Frequently throughout history we can see examples of powerful leaders giving one group rights at the expense of another group. In Britain the right to a health service open 24/7 and free at the point of delivery has been at the expense of the junior doctors. If you don't believe that, perhaps thinking that it is the nurses, those ministering angels, who provide health care you should read Adam Kay's book *"This Is Going To Hurt."* (Or perhaps two of my own. *The National Elf Service, Not The NHS* is very easy reading and there's my in-depth study: *Medicine, Money and Politics*.)

48

Junior Doctors have been forced to work very long hours (I regularly did 120 hours a week when I was a houseman), had their youth stolen from them, their private lives ruined, been paid appallingly badly and were not given the usual working rights that most people employed in Britain received. The doctors' vocational calling has been abused and now the managers have placed themselves firmly in charge in the hospitals and the consultants are receiving the same ill-treatment as the junior doctors.

That is just one example. Similar abuse is going on with regards to other workers in health care and is seen also in schools, higher education and in local councils.

So we have a trilogy: Rights, Power and Responsibility.

Rights can only be provided if someone in power finds someone to take responsibility for delivering those rights. Too frequently the people in power make a small group deliver the rights whilst pandering to the large mass that keep them in power.

The Last Rites?

So my final cartoon in this section? I thought I would bring in the priest delivering the last rites. You met him previously sitting on the pope's propaganda committee (page 11) and selling indulgences (page 28).

49

Section 3
Purveyors of Snake Oil

The strange name of this section refers to the controversy which still exists over the traditional Chinese medicine of snake oil. *Snake oil* is commonly associated with the US District Court judgment against Clark Stanley[1]. It is likely that their liniment contained no actual oil from snakes and was based mainly on mineral oil.

Snake oil salesmen are a standard figure in popular cowboy films about the Wild West. They are depicted as purveyors of fake medicine that has no active ingredients, working only by its placebo effect.

Throughout the history of medicine such quackery has been a common problem. A respected doctor would announce that they knew about the workings of the human body, explain their theory and convince people that they had a cure for a huge variety of ailments.

Much traditional medicine is based on this behaviour and has no basis in truth. In fact it is another example of fake news.

The King's Healing Touch

Charles II "healing" scrofula

The King's evil and the Royal Touch:
The Story of Scrofula [2]

For over seven hundred years it was widely believed that the kings of England and France could cure the condition known as scrofula with their royal gift of healing.

Scrofula is an enlargement of the cervical lymph nodes due to Tuberculosis or due to non-tuberculous (atypical) mycobacteria.

Shakespeare, in Macbeth Act IV Sc 3, has Malcolm say...
'Tis call'd the evil: A most miraculous work in this good king; Which often, since my here-remain in England, I have seen him do. How he solicits heaven, Himself best knows: but strangely-visited people, All swollen and ulcerous, pitiful to the eye, The mere despair of surgery, he cures, Hanging a golden stamp about their neck.' In the play Malcolm is referring to Edward the Confessor but the ceremony he described was that practised by James I.

Edward the Confessor was, however, the first king of England believed to touch for Scrofula. If he did indeed do so and if he gave a coin, which is doubtful, then the coin he would have given was a silver penny since this was the only coin minted in his reign. In later reigns the sufferer would stand in front of the King or Queen, the royal ruler would touch the patient, say a short blessing and give the person a coin, pronouncing them cured. The coin was then to be worn on a string round the person's neck. This made them acceptable in society but would, since it was totally ineffective as a cure, just tend to spread the infective disease.

The touching ceremony in England was stopped under Oliver Cromwell but Charles II restarted the touching ceremony and in his reign touched nearly 100,000 patients, giving each a gold coin.

As would be expected the incidence of scrofula increased

dramatically over the seven hundred year period. The touching ceremony was considered to be a great public relations success. Queen Anne (1665-1714) did not want to resurrect the touching ceremony when she came to the throne in 1702. William III had stopped the tradition but Anne was told that the public were demanding it so she obliged. Samuel Johnson was one of the last to be touched for scrofula. He continued to suffer from it for the rest of his life but his gold coin, a touchpiece, is in the British Museum.

Once the ceremony had been suspended in the UK other equally useless techniques and medicines were promulgated for the treatment of glandular and respiratory tuberculosis. Thus faith healers would try their luck and various spas were promoted for their healing waters, including the healing of scrofula.

Pigot's Directory of Gloucestershire, 1830, states:

"The Hotwells are situated about one mile and a half westward from Bristol in the parish of Clifton. The salutary spring rises near the bottom of the cliff, and so copious as to discharge 60 gallons in a minute. The water is warm as milk, and like those of Bath, famous for the cure of stone and gravel, diarrhoea, diabetes, King's evil, scrofula and cancers."

A second hot spring was discovered in Hotwells further down river. This was also promoted as a treatment for Tuberculosis and when John Wesley in 1754 developed *"Galloping Consumption"* he tried the waters of both wells and preferred the new well. It now feeds a drinking fountain adjacent to the Portway.

54

Quacks and their Cures

Quacks and their Cures is the alternative title for this entire section.

It arises from the Dutch term "quacksalver" [3,4]. Now spelled kwakzalver in the modern Dutch, this referred to a person who sold medicines. Presumably the term was used because quicksilver, or mercury, was one of the most important remedies on offer, being at the time the only known treatment for one of the most common and devastating conditions: syphilis. Eventually the term quack became attached to any person who provided unsatisfactory or unconventional treatment.

In view of the offer of spa water on the opposite page this might be a place to mention homeopathy. I like the comment by Adam Kay[5] that the only thing homeopathy cures is thirst. I am not going to pursue the subject as it has been done to death elsewhere.[6] My view is that it is useful to have a placebo that is relatively harmless as long as the patient does not avoid having effective treatment because they are on the placebo.

It was, of course, difficult to distinguish a bona-fide doctor from a quack in the past. The common treatments of purging and blood-letting did no end of harm. Add astrology to the mix and you have all the necessary ingredients for quackery. By the last century, however,, it should have been possible using good trials to tell whether treatments were fake news or were effective but still some dreadful examples of malpractice can be found.

Undoubtedly some of the worst were the Nazi doctors who experimented on prisoners in the German concentration camps. Josef Mengele[7] (1911-1979) was reputed to be one of the most odious and he performed many unethical

The fake news of Aryan Supremacy

operations, killing countless prisoners, in his attempts to bolster the false Nazi premise, the fake news, of the superiority of the Aryan race. He escaped to South America and evaded capture for the rest of his life, finally dying in 1979 from a stroke whilst swimming. His remains had to be exhumed in 1985 to counter the rumoured sightings of him from around the world.

Walter Freeman 1895 – 1972

American comic, Fred Allen (1894-1956), once succinctly quipped *"I'd rather have a full bottle in front of me than a full frontal lobotomy."* [8] He remarked in this way because the dire results of the technique were becoming apparent to everybody even by the early 1950s.

These two pages are about the "Father of the Lobotomy" Walter Freeman[9]. One of the most despicable and influential surgeons of the Twentieth Century Freeman was actually a physician rather than a surgeon. He was born in Philadelphia and practised in the USA but also performed and propagated his pet subject in Europe. The surgical technique was based on a procedure intended to treat mental illness, first performed in Portugal under the direction of neurologist and physician Egas Moniz. Moniz called it a "leucotomy" and it involved taking small corings out of the frontal lobes. [10]

Freeman simplified the procedure to the point where it simply consisted of disabling the person with an electric shock then hammering chisels into the frontal lobes via both the eye sockets. No imaging technique was used and the damage done was not quantified.

Not surprisingly the results were appalling with many of the patients dying or left with severe physical and mental disabilities. But Freeman travelled the world convincing people that his technique was for the good of the patients. Mental institutions clamoured for his procedure because it left the difficult patients in a much more docile state. Or dead!

Neurosurgeons in Europe were persuaded to undertake lobotomies, convinced by his published papers falsely showing remarkable improvement in severely mentally ill and disturbed patients.

Patients often had to be retaught how to eat and use the bathroom, some never recovered and about 15% died from the procedure. [11]

But still Freeman persisted with his technique even lobotomising children[12]. He performed 3,439 lobotomies during his career, vanishingly few of which were justified.[13]

Unfortunately this particular cartoon is not funny. It shows the technique Freeman used to lobotomise patients.

Twenty-first Century Quacks

It is a strange fact that as conventional western medicine has improved so has belief in alternative therapy.

Some of this can be considered as complementary to conventional treatment but much of the alternative therapy being offered is expensive, totally ineffective and directs people away from effective treatment.

One area rife with controversy is that of cancer treatment. There are now many sites on the internet where one can read about alternative therapy. One good site is that hosted by Cancer Research UK.[14]

"Natural is better": Cancer Research UK point out that many present medicines, such as Taxol, are derived from naturally occurring substances (yew leaves in the case of Taxol) but that many natural substances are highly toxic.

"Blogs of successful cases": Cancer Research UK cite the case of Belle Gibson who claimed to have cured herself of a brain tumour, only later to admit she had never had cancer at all. I have personally seen many cases where the patient claimed a cure based on ingestion of carrot juice or similar substances, completely ignoring the successful treatment they had received at the Oncology Centre.

But quite often complementary medicine does help, particularly in improving the morale of a patient. Much of this can be put down to the placebo effect but that is not in itself a bad thing. The placebo effect can be very beneficial for a patient. Unfortunately, because conventional treatment has many side effects, the patient has to be warned about the things that can go wrong and this can have the opposite to the placebo effect: the "nocebo" effect. This can actually harm a patient's health.

If you are thinking about having complementary medicine do research it thoroughly using websites that are bona fide and discuss it with your general practitioner and the hospital specialist.

Some alternative medicines are very powerful and harmful interactions with conventional medicines is possible. This is particularly true of herbal compounds, many of which have very potent constituents than can interere with other medicines.

Some forms of alternative medicine are completely bonkers. The Feedback page in New Scientist frequently remarks on examples of "fruitloopery" in advertised alternative medicine. The author of the column noted that.... *'along with "vibrational energies", combinations of the words "subtle", "energy", "quantum" and "physics" were sure-fire indicators that texts mentioning them were fruitloopery deluxe...* '[15]

Vaccination

When vaccination was discovered by Edward Jenner it was a revolution in medical treatment. For the first time in history we had a preventative procedure that was relatively harmless and protected the patient against a life-threatening disease.

Jenner is a hero of mine and his work led the way towards immunisation against a huge variety of diseases. But vaccination has not been without its critics. In recent years there has been a big drive against immunisation. The people who led this drive have been demonised by public health doctors, the GMC and other public bodies set up to protect our health. These organisations have quite rightly pointed out that some childhood diseases, such as measles, have made a comeback leading to minor epidemics and

some deaths. They have then reiterated the message that immunisation of all children is essential in order to prevent major epidemics and many deaths.

This is basically true but the argument is not as simple as they tend to suggest. All of the comments from the vaccinator in the cartoon above are lies. Immunisation may well hurt, it can have side effects, minor and major, and it rarely provides lifelong protection. Even vaccination with vaccinia against smallpox only provided individual immunity for about ten years. Despite this deficiency it has achieved the amazing result of eliminating smallpox. *(As long as it does not escape from one of the laboratories in the USA or Russia, see the cartoon on page 79. Ed.)*

So what are the benefits of vaccination? If the immunity of the community as a whole can be raised to sufficient levels "herd immunity" is achieved. In that situation even people who cannot be immunised, due to age or infirmity, can also be protected. The percentage of people who need to be immunised to reach such herd immunity varies depending on how contagious the disease is[16]. Measles, a very contagious disease, requires 90-95% of the population to be vaccinated. Some diseases, such as polio, are less contagious and require around 80-85% but this is still a high percentage given that some people cannot be immunised.

What can be done to increase the percentage of people being immunised? One idea would be to provide a no-faults compensation if the immunisation causes harm. Vaccination can, very, very occasionally, lead to encephalitis and brain damage. In such a situation it should not be necessary for the patient or their guardians to prove negligence...if the patient or parents had been warned about the side effect they would probably not win anyway. Compensation should be automatic if serious damage due to the immunistaion could be proved and negligence should not have to be cited.

Deciding whether you or your children should be immunised requres a decision in which the various benefits and harms are balanced against each other. In a free society when the disease has become rare people will not want the injections. To make people decide to have a vaccination requires honesty on the part of the vaccinators and compensation if something does go wrong.

Or perhaps simply paying them? But that raises another entire debate on the ethics of payment to patients, organ donors etcetera, and this is something which I do not wish to get into here. Maybe in the next cartoon book?

REFERENCES

1. *https://en.wikipedia.org/wiki/Snake_oil*
2. *The King's Evil. Paul R Goddard Bristol Medico-Historical Society Proceedings Volume 6 pages 56-61 Clinical Press Ltd. 2015*
3. *http://mentalfloss.com/article/33558/why-fake-doctor-called-quack*
4. *https://metro.co.uk/2017/08/17/why-are-doctors-called-quacks-and-where-did-the-nickname-come-from-6858852/*
5. *This is Going to Hurt: Secret Diaries of a Junior Doctor by Adam Kay*
6. *https://www.smithsonianmag.com/smart-news/1800-studies-later-scientists-conclude-homeopathy-doesnt-work-180954534/*
7. *https://en.wikipedia.org/wiki/Josef_Mengele*
8. *https://www.brainyquote.com/quotes/fred_allen_384342*
9. *McManamy J. Walter Freeman – father of the lobotomy. McMan's Depression and Bipolar Web website. Reviewed Jan. 15, 2011. http://www.mcmanweb.com/lobotomy.html*
10. *https://www.medicalbag.com/despicable-doctors/walter-freeman-the-father-of-the-lobotomy/article/472966/*
11. *https://en.wikipedia.org/wiki/Walter_Jackson_Freeman_II*
12. *Howard Dully; Charles Fleming (2007). My Lobotomy: A Memoir. Three Rivers Press. p. 66. Archived from the original on 2013-12-26*
13. *http://listverse.com/2009/11/10/10-unabashed-quacks-in-medical-history/*
14. *https://scienceblog.cancerresearchuk.org/2015/04/27/alternative-therapies-whats-the-harm/*
15. *Feedback 8th August 2007 New Scientist*
16. *https://www.ovg.ox.ac.uk/news/herd-immunity-how-does-it-work*

Section 4
Statistics and Science

Lying With Statistics

How to lie with Statistics is a little book (not quite as small as this but still quite short) written in 1954 by Darrell Huff. I had a copy on my bookshelf when I was first at university as it provided an introduction to statistics that is both informative and amusing.

His chapters have such self-explanatory titles as

1. The Sample with the Built-in Bias

2. The Well Chosen Average

3. The Little Figures That Are Not There

and many more.

For anybody wishing to read a simple guide to the mystifying world of statistical analysis just search for the book on Amazon.... there are plenty of copies available.

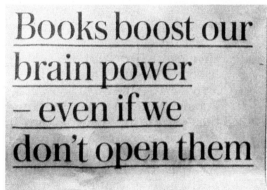

Books boost our
brain power
– even if we
don't open them

According to the headline in the Daily Telegraph (10th October 2018) you won't even have to read the book in order to have your intelligence boosted. But does that seem very likely? Several of our methods of detecting lies suggest that it is fake news. The headline employs alliteration, a good sign of demagoguery and also defies commonsense: how could books boost brain power if you don't open them? The opposite is true: *reading* books does boost brain power so it is unlikely that not reading them would also do so.

So where did the idea come from? Hannah Betts based it on a report published in Social Science Research. This study showed that the number of household books present when the subject was aged sixteen directly influenced their later literacy, numeracy and IT skills. The more books they grew up with, the better their brain power later. This was true whether the person read more than a person with fewer books or not.

So how can this be? Well, it is almost certainly an example of association being confused with causation. Households with more books are usually owned by people with a greater interest in education than homes with fewer books. It is likely that the adult interest will lead to a greater input on the children's education and the presence of numerous books will encourage the teenager to read more widely even if they do not read any more frequently.

So you will have to read the book if you want to benefit from it.

Spin

In 2002 I was involved in uncovering a massive example of spin propagated by the British Government. At the time we called it spin rather than fake news and the people who were in charge of pushing it out to the gullible public were known as spin doctors.

The Department of Health, the overall employer of most of the real doctors in the UK, assessed hospitals based on a star rating system, zero being the worst and three stars the best. People were given to believe that the hospitals with three stars (***) gave them the best service. Indeed this was going to be reflected in the first tranche of hospitals being offered Foundation Hospital status once the government managed to get the Foundation Hospital bill through Parliament.

Our local hospital group, which included the Bristol Royal Infirmary, my main place of employment, was rated as zero stars despite all our very determined efforts to provide the best possible care.

So I looked at the government's figures, the statistics collected from all over the country and referring to all aspects of health care. The clinical factors recorded mortality rates, patient complaints and readmission after surgery. The score for our hospital was twenty out of twenty (20/20): a perfect score that could not be bettered and one which was not matched by any other hospital group in England or Wales. So where had we fallen down?

That was soon discovered. We had overrun our budget.

What of other large teaching hospitals, were they suffering the same ignominy as ourselves? A famous teaching hospital on the opposite side of the country was an example. They had only scored ten out of twenty for clinical work *(oh dear)* but they had remained within budget so they were given three stars (***). They were widely being touted as the first group to be given Foundation Hospital status, thus giving the hospital greater autonomy and prestige!

I wrote to the national papers and my letter was published in the Daily Telegraph, followed by the Times, Financial Times etc. Questions were asked in parliament and our local MP,

The History of
Medicine,
Money
and Politics

Riding the Rollercoaster of State Medicine

Paul R Goddard M.D.

Valerie Davey, abstained from voting on the Foundation Hospital bill.

But it did no good. The bill was still passed and some of the worst hospitals, clinically, were rewarded with more money, more prestige and more independence.

In 2008 I wrote and published a book on the health service: *The History of Medicine, Money and Politics,* subtitled *Riding the Rollercoaster of State Medicine.*

This book featured in thirteen different newspapers, on TV and radio, including the Today programme *(no less!)* where I repeated my predictions of dire outcomes from bad treatment and poor conditions in some Foundation Hospitals.

Once again it did no good and the Stafford disaster and other similar catastrophes occurred.

The spin doctors with their fake news had been too successful and the government were continuing their policy of putting more money into management in the NHS whilst funds were being starved from the frontline staff.

The sub-prime mortgage financial collapse also occurred at the same time and the banks were bailed out to the tune of trillions of pounds. Suddenly the money that was not available for health care was peculiarly omnipresent for the banks. The lie had been exposed and failed bankers were bailed out and allowed to continue working on massive salaries and huge bonuses.

Have things improved since then?

The coalition government, 2010-2015, brought in "austerity" to pay for the bankers' transgressions (and their continuing undeserved bonuses). Hospital clinical staff had their pay effectively frozen. Perversely the chief executives of the hospitals were permitted to increase their own salaries at the rate of 25% per annum.

Some of this was mentioned in my book *The National Elf Service*. But again without avail.

This is another gratuitous plug for one of my books.

It is far too easy for governments to lie with statistics because the results are very seldom checked carefully *(if at all! Ed.)*

Economics and accountancy

The statement *"There is no science without measurement"* has been ascribed to Lord Kelvin. That does not, of course, mean that if there is measurement you definitely have a science: that would be arguing by inverted syllogism. (see page 25). Many times people have trusted very clever economics and marvellous mathematics only to find that the major and minor premises on which the calculations were based were fake. In recent years many people found that their faith in economic measurement has plummeted. As the Spectator noted in 2010 if the metrics (that is the measurements) are fiction, meaningful investment management is nigh impossible. [1] And that was the case in both 2001 and 2010. It has been estimated that the dot com bubble of 2001 cost investors $5 trillion [2] and in 2008 the subprime mortgage collapse cost the US economy at least $22 trillion [3].

Statistics have an ability to bamboozle even the most canny of readers. How many times have you skimmed over a series of calculations and graphs, accepting the explanations given but without checking the initial assumptions or calculating whether the results are correct? Frequently it is impossible to check the results.

Using statistics to detect fraud

I enjoy travelling by train. Compared with driving any distance train journeys are quieter, more relaxing and quicker. Their only drawback is the cost. At last the train companies in the UK are being made to simplify their ticket pricing and prudent use of a rail-card coupled with off-peak travel brings the cost to below that of the cost of petrol and parking. Today I travelled up to and back from London. On the way up I met a chap who told me that he had worked for the rail companies until recently and was travelling to a railway board meeting of some sort. He stated that he was very proud of the way that the trains had improved and the number of passengers they carried. I agreed that they now carried twice as many passengers as in the 1970s and 80s and that freight had also massively increased but I could not agree that they had necessarily improved. I referred to the fact that I could, forty years ago, travel up to London from Bristol Parkway in 59 minutes and that parking was free. Now you had to pay to park and you were lucky if the train got there in an hour and twenty minutes.

'I don't really know about that,' he replied. *'I never*

travelled by train then because I thought they were so bad. I suppose it is a matter of perception.'

Yes it is. The trains were really not bad at all in the 1980s but they were perceived as being so. Fake news had gripped them and they were privatised as a result.

On the Underground I asked a little old lady, travelling with her son of about my own age, whether she was going to have a good day in London.

'I'm off home now. I've had a great weekend,' she replied. *'It was a special treat for my birthday and I can only describe it as being magic.'*

Again, simply a matter of perception.

The next fellow I talked to, this time on the train returning home, was an expert on fraud in business. Fake news in accounting! But how do they detect it? With statistics, of course. When statistics are used properly they can give good results. But what is properly? It depends on who you are, the analyst or the fraudster. In this case the fraud detectors will analyse the accounts of myriads of businesses and look for the outliers. When fraud is committed the accounts will probably not look statistically like accounts that do not include fraud.

A short study of Benford's Law [4] is probably of value here as it applies to accounting fraud and to fraudulent results in medical and scientific papers.

Benford's law has several other names. It is also called Newcomb-Benford's law, the law of anomalous numbers, and first-digit law. It is about the frequency distribution of leading numbers in real-life measurements. The most common first or leading number in a set of numbers that follow a normal distribution is the number 1. This occurs in about 30% of cases but the number 9, in comparison, occurs less than 5%. If this distribution does not occur in a set of numbers, be they accounts or scientific results, then an explanation must be sought and frequently that explanation is fraud.

A massive example of such fraud detected by Benford's law is that of Greece[5]. Analysis shows that their government cheated in the figures they presented when joining the eurozone and afterwards.

Tim Worstall, writing for Forbes [5], states:

"Greece was lying about its budget numbers for years. First to get into the euro, then to cover up the damage it was having and more recently to avoid the difficult questions of what should be done about it....

According to Rauch and his colleagues, Greek data are further from the Benford distribution than that of any other European Union member state. Romania, Latvia and Belgium also have abnormally distributed data, while Portugal, Italy and Spain have a clean bill of health."

On that basis the Greek, Romanian, Latvian and Belgian economic data were fake news.

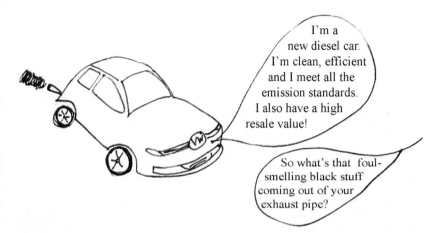

Fake Science

Purposely fraudulent science is a particularly bad thing because it misleads other scientists and policy makers. We don't really expect scientists to lie and bad science leads to a bad response.

A good example here is that of global warming. A while ago climatologists were apparently pushing the mantra that our problems were all due to excessive use of fossil fuels causing global warming via the emission of carbon dioxide. I have used the word "apparently" because close analysis of what they were saying showed that they were well aware of the fact that the problems are deeper than that. Other equally *(maybe more?Ed.)* important problems include destruction of rainforests, poisonous pollution of the land, rivers and seas, emission of other gases than CO_2 (methane, NOx etcetera) and plastic waste.

The public and the politicians only heard the words "Cabon Dioxide". In response the sale of diesel cars was promoted, aided and abetted by technicians in large car companies *(especially but not only VW)* who purposely cheated the scientific testing that was supposed to ensure that the cars would not produce toxic emissions.... And then went on to boast in a series of adverts that the cars were environmentally friendly, clean, efficient and had a high resale value! Now we have an excess of diesel vehicles clogging our towns and cities. The evil carbon smuts and nitrogen oxide waste from these fraudulently produced cars pollutes our atmosphere and will probably cause as many early deaths as that other great scientific polluter of our air, Thomas Midgley*.

* Wikipedia reminds us that Thomas Midgley (1889-1944), was an American scientist and inventor. His two most famous inventions are both now banned because they are dangerous for the world environment: the use of lead in petrol (gasoline) and the use of chlorofluorocarbons (CFCs) in refrigerators. Midgley was accidentally killed by something he was inventing.[7]

Climate change has created a whole load of fake news, both from those who believe in it and those who do not. I have been accused of being a "climate change denier" because I long ago stated that climate change could not solely be due to carbon dioxide and that bad science would lead to bad outcomes. As well as the problem of diesel cars (with their smuts and NOx) one other particular problem I pointed out was the use of wood burning stoves. I have such stoves in my house and they are there in case of emergency. I still remember the 1970s when there were major power cuts and if the electricity stops so does our central heating. But the stoves are not environmentally friendly and I have been telling people this for years. (Most notably at a meeting on the Isle of Skye when I pointed out how much pollution a wood burning stove, even a modern one, could put into the air. I was roundly told to shut up because the stoves were carbon neutral.)

Now we are told that half the air pollution in cities is due to diesel engines and the other half is down to wood burning stoves.

Next is a headline about beer. This is presently fake news because it is only a prediction and in the UK the variation in price is very dependent on the level of tax.

The Daily Telegraph Tuesday 16 October 2018

Price of a pint will soar due to climate change, say scientists

| 1960s | 1990s | Today |

Of course we *must* stop pumping the fumes from fossil fuels into our atmosphere but equally we must stop poisoning the land and the sea.

In Brazil they are cutting down rain forests in order to put hydro-electricity schemes on the Amazon. They hardly use solar power at all! It makes you want to weep.

REFERENCES

1. https://spectator.org/39403_metrics-deceit/
2. https://www.moneycrashers.com/dot-com-bubble-burst/
3. https://www.huffingtonpost.com/2013/02/14/financial-crisis-cost-gao_n_2687553.html?guccounter=1
4. https://en.wikipedia.org/wiki/Benford%27s_law
5. https://www.forbes.com/sites/timworstall/2011/09/12/greece-was-lying-about-its-budget-numbers/#5068b2062185
6. https://www.nytimes.com/2016/03/30/business/media/ftc-sues-volkswagen-over-diesel-car-ads.html
7. https://simple.wikipedia.org/wiki/Thomas_Midgley

Section 5

Politics: International, National and Local
(and including a polemic about managers!)

Politics, either international, national or local, is fraught with fake news. Lies fly backwards and forwards between political parties and nowadays are propagated immediately by Twitter, Facebook and other social media.

The European Union has legislated about clean air in cities. I consider this to be a very good thing as the air quality has been declining for some years. It would be terrrible if we went back to the pea-souper smogs of yester-year which were only cleaned up by the introduction of the clean air acts of the 1950s and 60s.

On the pretext that it would improve the air quality and thus meet the standard, Bristol brought in a city-wide speed limit of twenty miles per hour, down from the previous 30mph. Immediately the air quality worsened as motorists travelled around for longer, in lower gears. Now they are telling us that it was actually brought in to reduce accidents.

In order to persuade people to slow down they offered laser speed guns to the public. Presumably the people who agreed to take up such activities are the same nosy neighbours who poke around in next door's recycyling bins.

You may wonder what a "nostrum" is. One meaning is a fake medicine but another is a scheme or remedy for social or political reform.

The Law of the Dialectic

It is my contention that a virtual dictatorship by managerial diktat has spread throughout the democratic western world. I believe that this is perversely the result of the fall of the USSR, East Germany and other communist regimes and of the various right wing dictatorships. Previously the democracies saw themselves as being different from either the left or right wing dictatorships. We were free speaking, liberal democracies. With the fall of our enemies we no longer have to define ourselves in this way and have instead absorbed ideas from all the regimes. From East Germany we have absorbed the ideas of the Stasi.... our local government now encourages people to check on their neighbours' noise levels and look in their bins to check that they are doing their correct recycling. The council will even issue laser speed guns to willing nosy-neighbour amateurs. From all the dictatorships we have taken the notion that micro-management of everybody's working lives by line management leads to efficiency. Yet this was clearly not the case in any of the dictatorships and they all suffered from chronic inefficiency. Letting the professionals manage themselves has always led to the greatest success and trying to micro-manage in areas as complex as medicine is a total disaster.

So why did this absorption of ideas occur? Hegel, Engels and Marx would have suggested that this is a natural result of the Law of the Dialectic [1]. They postulated that any initial idea, which they called the the thesis, would have an opposite, the antithesis. When the two arguments meet a third idea emerges as a result. This final idea is known as the synthesis and the process is the law of the dialectic. Whilst there is no doubt that such laws are too simplistic they do contain an element of truth. Simply as a result of the fall of the dictatorships the spread of their philosophies and systems was inevitable. This seems to have found fertile ground amongst the managerial classes who enjoy telling people what to do even when they themselves do not know what they are talking about.

Is there any way of combating this? Perhaps not but it might be fruitful to establish a register for managers so that they are subject to the same stringent codes of practice as professionals.

What Is wrong with the Management Process?

Why is the management process so inimical to the role of the professional? Wikipedia [2] defines the Managerial Process as "a process of setting goals, planning and/or controlling the organising and leading the execution of any type of activity." The key word that explains the difference between management and the professional is the word "any". It is the firmly held view of the purveyors of the dreaded MBA (Master of Business Administration) that a manager does not have to understand the business of which he or she is in charge in order to manage it. The process, they say, is the same in every business and every type of human activity can be considered as a business. Thus the manager can be placed in charge of anyone or everyone even though they do not have the skills of the workforce under them.

Hence, armed with their MBA certificate, untrained managers can lord it over highly trained professionals. Of course it is just fake news. Managers cannot efficiently manage any business

So what are these people doing?

Some sort of genetic experiment I believe.

But you are their manager. Don't you know exactly what they are doing?

The management process is the same whatever they are doing. I don't have to understand their work in order to manage them.

I'm closing you down. There is a breach of Health and Safety. They are not using the correct protection procedures.

See the old geezer in the white coat? That's his responsibility, not mine.

if they do not understand it.

So this takes us right back to page 49 and the severing or rights, responsibilities and power. Managers are taking the power but not shouldering the responsibility.

You can see this in international and national politics also. Who can forget the look of surprise on Boris Johnson's face

Boris Johnson in a remake of the Italian Job?

when they won the Brexit (Leave the EU) vote? Or the jaunty way that David Cameron stepped away from the mess he had made, a little tune emanating from his lips. They wanted the power but they did not want the responsibility.

Almost all the leaders of the British political parties stepped down from leadership just when the country needed them most.

The continuing mess under Theresa May has thrown up some very unlikely candidates for leadership of the Conservative Party. Jacob Rees-Mogg (see opposite) is one example.

The Labour party is led by the far-left MP for Islington North, Jeremy Corbyn. He has tried to remake his image away from the hard left policies he has formerly espoused. But do not be fooled!

Certainly the trickle-down idea of letting the rich get richer and allowing the extra money to leech down to the poor is very attractive to wealthy people but has not worked. There are more people sleeping rough and falling out of society than ever before and the life expectancy has stopped rising in the United Kingdom.

I have great sympathy with the idea of supporting poor people but the hard left Labour response of attacking the so-called rich just impoverishes everybody. This has been shown historically. A tax on large houses would hit retired people most and would probably not affect the rich at all.

Insisting that large international firms pay a fair amount of tax and encouraging employment of people presently on benefits would seem to be a better approach.

Chancellor has discovered a magic money tree on Planet Tory

The Daily Telegraph correspondent (30.10.18) thought that the budget to end austerity was unlikely to succeed. Just another prediction, really.

The boys were just on holiday

And here is somebody else who knows a thing or two about left wing politics. I think he must be referring to the men who tried to murder the Skripals, an attempt that led to the death of Dawn Sturgess

Oh dear, he was lying and has now changed into a collared lizard.

More fake news!

Who would have thought it?

Fake news!

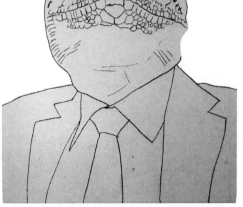

The politicians are not all as we think they are and certainly not what they would like us to think they are!

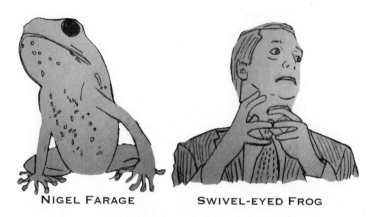

NIGEL FARAGE　　　　SWIVEL-EYED FROG

Is Nigel really a swivel-eyed amphibian and Tony an alligator? No, of course they're not. *(Are you sure? Ed.)*

TONY BLAIR　　　　ALLIGATOR

Yes, I'm sure they're not and Theresa May is not a colour-changing chameleon. I know that for a fact because she's a robot! Just kidding: it's all fake news. Oh, now she's doing a silly dance and that's *not* fake news!

REFERENCES

1. *https://en.wikipedia.org/wiki/Dialectic*
2. *https://en.wikipedia.org/wiki/Management_process*

85

Section 6. Religion

Is Lying a Sin?

Tom Leherer use to sing a song about a young woman who killed all her family, even serving them up in an Irish stew. But when at last the police came by her murderous ways she could not deny *"for lying she knew was a sin."*

Then there's the famous song from the 1930s

Be sure it's true

When you say I love you

It's a sin to tell a lie.

But are they right? And does that mean that all fake news is a sin?

In Section 1 we explored the possibility of a world without fiction; a very much reduced world indeed. So do the religions even teach that lying is a sin? If you ask most laymen this question they will agree with the songs and the more savvy might even cite the ten commandments as found in the Holy Bible and the Hebrew scriptures.

We will ignore for a minute whether or not sin is something we wish to accept as existing and argue our case on the basis of the evidence of the religions being cited.

Careful analysis reveals that the ten commandments do not explicitly state that lying is sinful. The commandment that comes closest to one forbidding the act of lying is number 9.

"Thou shalt not bear false witness against thy neighbour."

(Exodus 20 vs 16)

There is a similar command in the Quran

Conceal not evidence; for whoever conceals it,- His heart is tainted with sin. (The Noble Quran, 2:283)

This, a very specific type of lie, is forbidden. What it tells you is that purposely putting your neighbour in trouble by lying in court is a sin. Thus if the nosy neighbour, Mrs. Nostrum, lied to the council about next door's rubbish and hence stirred up trouble against them it would be a major break of the Christian, Jewish and Islamic commandments.

Not everybody is your neighbour and therefore not everybody is protected by this commandment.

I want, however, to disagree with the commandments. There may be many occasions where it would be morally wrong to tell the truth even if the person in question is your neighbour and you may be getting them into trouble.

In the cartoon a mad axeman has arrived at your door. He wants to chop off your wife's head and asks whether or not she is at home. To say yes would be to invite her demise, to say no would be a lie as you are fully aware that she is upstairs taking a well-earned nap. Simple morality and commonsense tells you that your duty is to your wife, not to the mad axeman, even if he happened to be your neighbour. Point the way towards the police station and tell him that she has just gone out for a short walk!

Fake News can be very funny. The Sunday Sport amused me recently with a fake news story, plus photographs, asserting that Theresa May is a robot. It was a lie, it was fake news but it was a very funny article. It was not a sin. Alternatively Fake News can be very dangerous leading to mob rule and even in this enlightened era (*enlightened? Ed.*) stir hatred and violence. People have been burned to death because of a rumour on WhatsApp![1] Exploring the idea of sin, it is clear that you usually need a religion if you are to have a concept of sin as being an immoral act transgressing divine law. Can we develop a similar concept without invoking divine law? I believe that we can and it would include mindless mob rule, pollution, wasteful behaviour and purposeful desecration of nature. Thomas Midgley comes to mind again and his development of lead in petrol and CFCs. In our new version of sin he would not be in Hell, though perhaps he deserves to be there.

REFERENCES

1. https://www.bbc.co.uk/news/world-latin-america-46145986

Faith, Hope and Love

And now we have faith, hope and love but the greatest of these is love. 1 Corinthians 13, 13 The Holy Bible

Regional elections in Indonesia

Voting for God

TASIKMALAYA
No one wants to get on the wrong side of Islamic zealots

The Economist April 14th 2018

I am not going to state whether present day religions are right or wrong. That would be far too dangerous in today's climate. The purpose of this book has been to encourage people to think for themselves and to do so in a reasoned manner so I shall leave the judgement up to the reader.

However I will point out that there are many religions and they all disagree adamantly with each other. They differ on most things but particularly the existence of gods. Jainism and Buddhism do not really promote the idea of a creator or god, Islam and Judaism claim there is one god and Christianity posits three-in-one , the Holy Trinity. One of the three is the *"Only begotten Son" (of God)* (John 3 vs.16 AV) but a few verses in the Christian holy text (the Bible) refer to multiple sons of God, for example Job 2 vs 1AV:

Again there was a day when the sons of God came to present themselves before the Lord

Hindus believe in many gods and there are numerous other religions that accept multiple deities and spirits.

Since the ideas are mutually exclusive they cannot all be right. It is therefore clear that religions are stashed full of fake news. We should ask ourselves why religion is such a fertile ground for fake news.

Inherent in most religions is the tenet that you should accept what is put forward as fact and do so using faith. So what is faith and why is it so problematical? Is not faith supposed to be, with love and hope, the most important of our emotions?

The Pages dictionary states:

Faith is:

1 complete trust or confidence in someone or something:
Example:*this restores one's faith in politicians.*

2 strong belief in the doctrines of a religion, based on spiritual conviction rather than proof: Example:*bereaved people who have shown supreme faith.*

The dictionary also states that to keep faith is to be loyal and to break faith is to be disloyal.

It is the complete confidence and the lack of proof that is the problem with faith. People who push faith as more important than anything else run the risk of denigrating the human intelligence and the necessity of questioning statements, testing the credibility and seeking proof. If you do that you are being disloyal!   Thus all of the tests put forward in chapter 1 of this book must be avoided if you are to be a true and loyal follower of a faith.

The importance of faith is recorded in the Bible.

"I tell you the truth, if you have faith as small as a mustard seed, you can say to this mountain, 'move from here to there' and it will move; Nothing will be impossible for you" (Matthew 14 verses 17-20)

In Christianity the elevation of belief above anything else was historically propagated by Calvin and is pursued by some of the Protestant versions of that religion and by the

more militant Islamists. The difficulty with this is that love and hope, otherwise put forward as extremely important, might be pushed into abeyance by those pursuing faith at all costs. Saint Paul would not have approved!

Am I saying that faith is all bad? Not at all. There are times when it is necessary to trust things: to have faith in our own judgement, to trust our partner, to believe in a cause. But to do so continuously and unquestioningly does permit fake news to dominate our lives.

Having been seventeen years of age in the *Summer of Love* of 1967 I enjoyed making the next cartoon.

Of course it is an example of fake news...we do need a little more than just love but it certainly helps.

Now a spoiler alert for the next cartoon. Don't tell the kids!

The picture is entitled *Father Christmas Is On His Way*.

Yes, I'm sorry to say that it is fake news. We've been telling our children and grandchildren a pack of lies but do enjoy the lies while you can!

Trump gets the last words after all.

Fake news!